HUMP[...]
REPT[...]

Laura Mayer

SHIRE PUBLICATIONS

Published in Great Britain in 2014 by Shire Publications Ltd, PO Box 883, Oxford, OX1 9PL, UK.

PO Box 3985, New York, NY 10185-3985, USA.

E-mail: shire@shirebooks.co.uk www.shirebooks.co.uk

A CIP catalogue record for this book is available from the British Library.

Shire Library no. 768. ISBN-13: 978 0 74781 294 4
PDF ISBN 978 0 74781 529 7
ePub ISBN 978 0 74781 528 0

Laura Mayer has asserted her right under the Copyright, Designs and Patents Act, 1988, to be identified as the author of this book.

Designed by Tony Trucott Designs, Sussex, UK and typeset in Perpetua and Gill Sans.

Printed in China through Worldprint Ltd.

14 15 16 17 18   10 9 8 7 6 5 4 3 2 1

COVER IMAGE
Repton's Regency style celebrated industrialisation and artifice. The beauty of this formal design for a Thames-side villa near London came, he argued, specifically from its proximity to the capital. (The Stapleton Collection/ The Bridgeman Art Library)

TITLE PAGE IMAGE
Repton transformed Hatchlands, Surrey, into a 'Gentleman-like residence in the midst of a park' by screening it from the road with trees. His dressed lawns and gravel walks survive today. *National Trust*

CONTENTS PAGE IMAGE
Jane Austen famously satirised devotees of the Picturesque 'with all the eagerness of real taste' in *Northanger Abbey*. This image of a fashionable party surveying Longleat was included in the 1803 Red Book for the 2nd Marquess of Bath.

ACKNOWLEDGEMENTS
Like Repton, I relied heavily upon my own breviary of four. I therefore owe a great debt to Richard Aitken, Timothy Mowl and Michael Richardson for their encouragement and wise counsel, and to Christopher Gibson, who supported this venture whilst managing our own Clifton 'improvements'. Warm thanks are due to Dianne Barre, Jane Bradney, Diane James and Marion Mako, who willingly lent their expertise. This book is dedicated to Viv Sykes.

IMAGE ACKNOWLEDGEMENTS
I would like to thank the following for permission to reproduce pictures:

Architectural Association Library, pages 10, 21 (bottom), 48 (bottom); Burleigh House Collection/The Bridgeman Art Library, page 4; Gloucestershire Archives (D/1571, E396), page 29 (all); Hereford City Library, page 38 (all); The National Trust, pages 1, 6/7 (bottom), 30, 44 (all), 54 (top); Trustees of the William Salt Library (SV-IV.20), page 6 (top); University of Bristol Special Collections, pages 8, 20, 36, 40, 43 (bottom), 52 (top and middle), 54 (bottom), 55–7 (all).

I am particularly grateful for the kindness of those listed below, in allowing the generous publication of images from their collections: Richard Aitken, page 58; Allport Library and Museum of Fine Arts, Tasmanian Archive and Heritage Office, page 60 (bottom); Botanic Gardens of Adelaide, pages 3, 9, 11 (all), 39 (all), 43 (top), 45 (all), 48 (top), 50, 60 (top); The Davenport Family, page 7 (top); Hotel Endsleigh, pages 52 (bottom), 53 (all); Timothy Mowl, pages 21 (top), 27, 28, 32; Sir Michael and Lady Nourse, photographs by Val Corbett, pages 25 (top), 26; Private Collectors, pages 31, 34/35 (all), 37 (all); State Library of Victoria, pages 14, 16–19 (all), 42 (all), 46, 49, 51 (all), 59 (bottom); Stoneleigh Abbey Ltd, pages 13, 22, 25 (bottom), 59 (top); and Sir Richard Baker Wilbraham, page 24 (all).

Shire Publications is supporting the Woodland Trust, the UK's leading woodland conservation charity, by funding the dedication of trees.

CONTENTS

INTRODUCTION: BROWN'S LEGACY

O N 6 February 1783, Lancelot 'Capability' Brown called upon his old friend and patron Lord Coventry in Piccadilly. Returning home he had a fit, fell to the ground and died almost immediately. He was sixty-seven years old. 'Your dryads must go into black gloves', Horace Walpole announced dramatically to Lady Ossory. 'Their father-in-law, Lady Nature's second husband, is dead!' Certainly, Brown's life had been one exhaustive journey, travelling the length and breadth of the country in a bid to reduce the English countryside to a simple pastoral idyll, one landscaping scheme at a time. A ruthlessly ambitious businessman, Brown rose from apprentice under-gardener at a modest Northumbrian estate to the lofty position of Master Gardener to George III. At his death, 170 great estates had been shaped for leisure, profit and sport by his personal design, while over 4,000 landscape parks had been created by a new generation of natural landscapists inspired by him.

As late as 1800, an anonymous pamphleteer, describing Brown's work at Fisherwick Hall in Staffordshire, observed that 'his genius has afforded such proofs of true taste in nature's beauties, as seemed unknown before his time'. Landscape minimalism had triumphed, but the century's relationship with nature was about to change. For, despite the aesthetic elegance and economic viability of a Brownian park, his repetitive formula began to grate with the average garden visitor, who missed the stylistic diversity supplied by the Arcadian layouts of the mid eighteenth century.

The garden tourist Mrs Lybbe Powys lamented that, because of Brown, 'every fine place throughout England is comparatively alike', as 'the rage for laying out grounds makes every nobleman and gentleman a copier of their neighbour'.

With the dawning of a new Romantic sensibility a band of Picturesque theorists emerged from the shadows, headed by Richard Payne Knight (1751–1824) and Sir Uvedale Price (1747–1829). These men despised Brown's parks as being artificial, lifeless and bland, and were not afraid to say so. 'I very earnestly wish that I might die before you,' snapped Richard

Opposite:
The pastoral idylls laid out by Lancelot 'Capability' Brown (1716–83) continue to be recognised as quintessentially English. It was said that he could assess the 'capabilities' of a particular terrain with only a circuit on horseback.

This 1786 watercolour of Fisherwick by James Spyers records Brown's Palladian house and graceful parkland, designed and built for Arthur Chichester. The garden marquees housed the 'elegant entertainments' responsible for Chichester's bankruptcy.

Owen Cambridge to Brown, 'because I should like to see heaven before you can improve it.'

In the midst of this bitter stylistic warfare, one man, Humphry Repton, set himself up as Brown's champion and self-styled successor. It was a bold

move, and one that would, unwittingly, open him up to sustained persecution from the Picturesque crusaders.

This book charts Repton's career as a landscape gardener as he struggled to reconcile his own personal ambitions and theoretic principles within the fluctuating tastes of the turn of the nineteenth century. It examines his extensive writings about the theory and practice of landscape gardening, and considers how both his style and social identity fluctuated and evolved. For, although Repton began by replicating almost exactly the manicured parkscapes of his idol, he was soon under pressure to produce the more wild and rugged 'savage Picturesque' landscapes advocated by Payne Knight and Price. By the beginning of the nineteenth century, Repton had been forced to abandon Brown's aesthetic altogether, as the fashion for landscape shifted from rough-hewn Picturesque

wildernesses to modest, suburban gardens with fussy flowerbeds and formal features. Here at last Repton came into his own, achieving with his Gardenesque style an uneasy compromise between Brown's bare lawns and the variety of the Picturesque.

Sir Uvedale Price, one of the leading proponents of the Picturesque aesthetic.

Left: Brown's seductive formula of aesthetic elegance and economic viability gave hundreds of country houses a sweeping view of lawn, lake and perimeter woodland. This is Berrington in Herefordshire.

REINVENTING REPTON

A portrait of Humphry Repton, commissioned for his *Fragments on the Theory and Practice of Landscape Gardening.*

Humphry Repton (1752–1818) was thirty-six years old with a raft of failed ventures behind him when he recreated himself as a 'landscape gardener' (a term he personally coined) in a bid to support his family. It would be a rocky journey from minor Norfolk squire to Capability Brown's eventual successor. Yet, once established, thanks largely to his competence as a watercolourist, Repton prevailed as the country's leading landscape gardener for thirty years. Although his ideas were frequently challenged, he dominated the development of the country house and its grounds in the late eighteenth and early nineteenth centuries, his influence overseas extending even beyond that.

In common with Brown, his lodestar, Repton was given hundreds of commissions, including such important estates as Woburn Abbey, Bedfordshire; Wimpole Hall, Cambridgeshire; Harewood House, West Yorkshire; and Holkham and Sheringham, in Norfolk. Both Brown and Repton were concerned with the architecture of a house, as well as its setting, and for his part Repton worked frequently with architects William Wilkins, John Nash and, later, his eldest son, John Adey Repton.

From his family background to his early career, Repton's start in life could not have been more different to Brown's. Yet, despite his advantages of birth and a classical education, he was never able to replicate his predecessor's breezy familiarity with the aristocracy

– the result of natural disposition and practical gardening ability – and instead felt awkward and out of place.

Repton was born in Bury St Edmunds, Suffolk, on 21 April 1752 to the moderately prosperous John and Martha Repton. His father was a tax collector and his mother the daughter of a minor Suffolk squire, John Fitch of Moor Hall. When Repton was ten years old the family moved to Norwich, where he attended the local grammar school. It was here that he met and befriended the botanist James Edward Smith. Destined from an early age for the thriving Norwich textile industry, in 1764 Repton was sent to Holland to learn Dutch under the tutelage of Zachary Hope of Rotterdam. He felt his separation from home keenly, but the Hopes were one of Holland's leading families and he soon 'learnt to take his place in society with an easy manner and quiet enjoyment which was to be invaluable to him in later years'.

On his return, Repton, now sixteen, embarked rather grudgingly on an apprenticeship in the textile industry. Once this was completed he married Mary Clarke in May 1773 and set up business in Norwich. Responsible for a rapidly growing family, Repton was forced to persevere with his mercantile career despite being an ineffective businessman. He soldiered on until the combined threat of financial ruin and the death of both his parents provided him with the escape route he so desperately wanted. Repton gave up his foundering business and, in 1778, bought a small country estate at Sustead, near Aylsham in Norfolk, where he dedicated himself to farming, socialising and indulging his passions for music, reading, writing and sketching. It was during this time that he befriended three of the leaders of Norfolk's agricultural reform movement: Nathaniel Kent, author of the influential *Hints to Gentlemen of Landed Property*, William Marshall, the estate manager at nearby Gunton, and Robert Marsham, a keen naturalist.

Money, however, was tight. When another friend and neighbour, William Windham of Felbrigg Hall, was appointed chief secretary to the Lord Lieutenant of Ireland in 1783, Repton jumped at the chance to accompany him as secretary. Unfortunately for Repton, his taste of the Dublin high life was to be a brief one as Windham resigned almost immediately. Determined to be cheerful, Repton wrote to warn Mary of his imminent return: 'I have made some valuable acquaintances; I have formed some connexions with the great.' It was this unfailing optimism and dogged determination in the face of adversity that would carry Repton through his career.

This vignette of a scroll dedicated to the art of landscape gardening illustrates Repton's belief in 'the united powers of the landscape painter and the practical gardener'.

Repton had turned his hand to various different professions – country squire, merchant, essayist, political secretary – all without success or financial remuneration. He resolved to reinvent himself one final time. In 1788, after a sleepless night, he made his decision: to become a landscape gardener. Repton wasted no time in touting for business and to this end sent out 'circular letters addressed to former friends' promoting his services:

> H. REPTON having for many years (merely as an amusement) studied the picturesque effect resulting from the art of LAYING OUT GROUNDS, has lately been advised by many respectable friends (to whom he has occasionally given sketches for the improvement of their own places) to enlarge his plan, and pursue professionally his skill in LANDSCAPE GARDENING.

Repton's Keeper's Cottage for Hooton Hall in Cheshire was influenced by William Kent. The squat Palladian building was to house hot and cold baths, and reinforced Repton's desire to bring 'inhabitancy' back into the landscape.

Justifying his credentials, these tradecards stated that 'Mason, Gilpin, Whately and Girardin have been of late my breviary – and the works of Kent, Brown and Richmond have been the places of my worship.' Certainly he took his new role seriously, visiting William Kent's gardens at Oatlands and Stowe, and Brown's landscapes at Blenheim, Holkham and Redgrave in the first instance.

By this time, Sustead, that relatively self-sufficient 'little earthly paradise', had proven beyond the family's limited means and had to be given up. Sometime around 1786, Repton leased the estate and moved his

The view from Repton's cottage in Hare Street village before he made extensive changes. Eyesores include beggars, an unused grass verge, wild fowl, ogling passers-by and hanging joints of meat.

family into a small cottage at Hare Street in Essex, which formed part of Richard Benyon's Gidea Hall estate. Intended as a temporary residence, Repton grew attached to this small, economical house and lived happily there until his death. Although comfortably well off, he would never amass the great wealth Brown accrued in later years. Over time, Repton lavished 'improvements' upon the cramped home, transforming it with *treillage* (trelliswork) and striped canvas awnings into a *cottage ornée*. It formed, in his own words, 'the most interesting subject I have ever known'.

In 1788, the year his childhood friend Smith founded the Linnean Society, Repton took on his first paid commission as a landscape gardener

After careful attention, pedestals overflowing with flowers and herbaceous borders gave Hare Street's extended garden a feeling of gentility. Repton did not banish all the traffic as he loved people.

at Catton Hall, near Norwich, for a wealthy merchant named Jeremiah Ives. He never looked back. At last his star was in the ascendant and financial security within reach. By 1795 he had worked on over fifty landscaping projects and, by his own account, more than 400 by the end of his career. Even before he died, Repton was immortalised in print, appearing in Jane Austen's *Mansfield Park* of 1814 and Thomas Love Peacock's *Headlong Hall*, published two years later. In *Mansfield Park*, the blundering Mr Rushworth attempts to impress Miss Bertram with his taste in landscape:

> 'Smith's place is the admiration of all the country; and it was a mere nothing before Repton took it in hand. I think I shall have Repton.'

Austen based the fictitious Mansfield Park on Stoneleigh Abbey in Warwickshire, the ancestral home of her mother and on which Repton produced a Red Book for Thomas Leigh in 1809.

In *Headlong Hall*, Repton appears in a less favourable light as the caricatured Marmaduke Milestone, boasting to Squire Headlong that his 'rocks shall be blown up, the trees shall be cut down, the wilderness and all its goats shall vanish like mist'. In place of these Picturesque monstrosities, a plethora of 'pagodas and Chinese bridges, gravel walks and shrubberies, bowling greens, canals and clumps of larch' should rise upon their ruins.

On 29 January 1811, Repton accompanied his daughters to a ball at Belhus, Essex, given by Sir Thomas Barrett Leonard, for whom he had worked four years previously. Returning to Hare Street via perilously icy roads, the Reptons' carriage overturned, tumbling the trio into the night. Mary and Elizabeth escaped unscathed, but the accident was to leave Repton semi-paralysed and wheelchair-bound for the rest of his life. John Adey (1775–1860) and his brother George Stanley Repton (1786–1858) managed the ongoing commissions as best they could under their father's direction, but Repton's increasingly frail health would permit only one last project and one final remodelling. The former was Sheringham Hall in Norfolk, recently purchased by a Mr and Mrs Upcher. Plans were completed in 1812, Repton believing the site offered 'more of what my predecessor called *Capabilities*' than any previous estate had provided, and John Adey began work on the Upchers' new villa that very year. Never one for false modesty, the ailing Repton happily found in his creation 'such a specimen of my art as I never before had an opportunity of displaying ... This may be considered my most favourite work: therefore I may say of it *exegi monumentum*'.

Ill health confined Repton's last efforts for the Earl of Bridgewater at Ashridge, Hertfordshire, to the immediate environs of the house. In a fit of whimsy, in 1813 he declared his work there as being 'the child of my age and declining powers'. Yet even in his final years Repton kept an eye on the main chance, writing optimistically that 'when no longer able to undertake the more extensive plans of *landscape* I was glad to contract my views within the narrow circle of the *garden*, independent of its accompaniment of distant scenery'.

Repton's condition deteriorated, and on 24 March 1818, he died in the arms of his servant while trying to reach the Hare Street breakfast table. His grave at Aylsham Church was planted with roses according to the lines etched on the stone, written himself explicitly for this purpose:

While its vivid blossoms cheer mankind
Its perfum'd odour shall ascend to heaven.

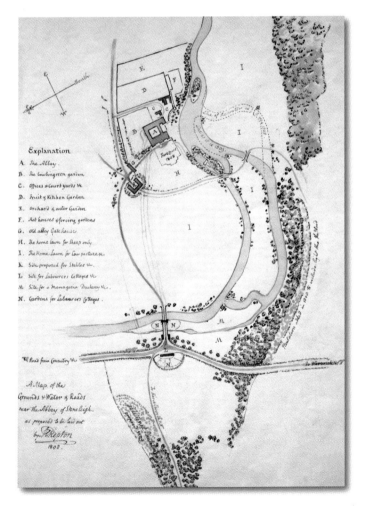

Repton's proposed remodelling of the formal grounds around Stoneleigh Abbey (Warwickshire) involved the realignment of the river and the creation of a new carriage drive from the Coventry road.

THE RED BOOKS

For the sensitive and snobbish Repton, laying out grounds was never just about gardening, nor did it stem from a patriotic wish to improve the English countryside. Rather, he was desperately seeking a way to ingratiate himself within aristocratic circles, while simultaneously raising the status of his adopted profession.

He believed, conveniently, that the art of laying out grounds could only be achieved by 'the united powers of the *landscape painter* and the *practical gardener*', and in this ingenious way combined his basic knowledge of farming gleaned at Sustead with his talent for topographical sketching. Consequently his famous Red Books, intended to help clients visualise the potential of their estates, encouraged an appreciation of landscape aesthetics while allowing their deferential creator access to the higher echelons of society.

Repton's Red Books, so-called because of their scarlet leather binding, were an undeniable stroke of sales genius. 'My habit of landscape sketching I have considerably improved by practice and this may be of great use in shewing effects where descriptions are not sufficient,' he wrote. Essentially, the Red Book was a detailed and persuasive contract for improvements, illustrated with seductive 'before and after' snapshots of the estate in question.

With a hinged overlay in place, the prospective client saw a watercolour illustration of his property and grounds; once this was lifted he was able to picture immediately the effects a new design could achieve, should he choose to employ the services of Repton. These watercolours were accompanied by explanatory text and engineered to convince prospective customers of the merit of his designs. Their theoretical methodology differed greatly from Brown's, who rarely wrote about his landscapes and relied only on large-scale plans drawn up by his surveyors, Samuel Lapidge and John Spyers. As Stephen Daniels has argued in his definitive study, *Humphry Repton: Landscape Gardening and the Geography of Georgian England*, Repton recognised that in order to succeed Brown he would need to pare down the contracting side of the business and supplement the consultancy.

Opposite:
This Red Book illustration for Brighton Pavilion is typically peopled with idling gentlefolk, enjoying the luxury of leisure, and royal groomsmen collecting water for the nearby stables.

Next spread: The Prince of Wales lavished funds on the pursuit of pleasure. Repton was first consulted over Brighton Pavilion in 1797, delivering a Red Book in 1806. These designs for the view from the 'pavillon' exemplify the power of his before-and-after sketches. Repton's vision for Brighton Pavilion transformed the grounds surrounding the royal residence into an exotic and flamboyant playground.

This outline shews the heights of the Trees as they appeared in Winter, forming three distinct distances; it also shews the relative height of a Man with a Rod of Ten feet long at different stations.

This Building was totally hid by the Trees near the Pavillion, some of which have been removed.

The farther Avenue remaining.

The first Avenue Cut down.

A great number of Young Trees stood here, some of which are removed to the same distance on the other side of the Town, as there represented.

Repton collaborated with his sons, John Adey and George Stanley, on his designs for Brighton Pavilion. His Red Book showcased William Porden's imposing Indian-style riding house, shown here in the 'before' sketch.

Brown's phenomenal success as a landscape designer was the combined result of three attributes: hard-headed business sense, a practical grasp of gardening and the ability to reconcile agricultural and sporting pursuits within a harmonious landscape. Repton's would be his tenacity, his unfailing desire to please, and his Red Books, an artistic achievement in their own right. Unfortunately, these also contributed to his financial pressures. Working as a consultant and charging for the manuscript documents, without necessarily overseeing the installation of their designs, meant that many commissions went unexecuted.

Repton's 'after' sketch with a view of Porden's riding house. When the Prince of Wales declared that Repton's plans 'far exceeded his expectations', Repton basked in 'the highest point of my ambition, in conjunction with my boys'.

When he presented the Duke of Bedford with his Red Book for Endsleigh, Repton hoped 'that my plans will not (as I have too often experienced) be a waste of Time, Thought and Contrivance'. A Red Book came to be seen as a finished work in its own right and copies were often displayed proudly, their owners having no intention of carrying out their designs. Worse still, with detailed written instructions and precise drawings, the Red Books often rendered Repton redundant, as owners could carry out his improvements using their own, cheaper, garden labourers. This was the case at Rode Hall, south-west of Congleton in Cheshire, where the work was given to John Webb, a pupil of the landscape

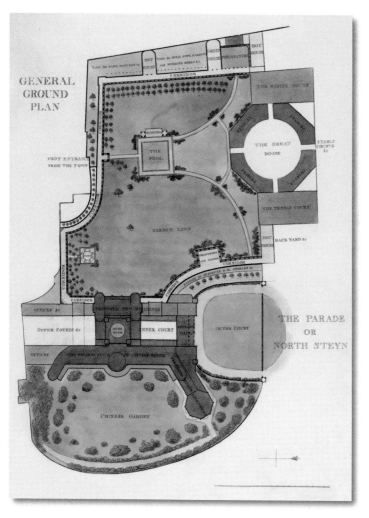

Hopes for Brighton Pavilion were 'like a brilliant bubble burst and vanished into the air'. Repton was unceremoniously dropped from the project in favour of John Nash, his ground plan abandoned at the publishers.

gardener William Emes. Consequently, the Baker Wilbraham family have a Red Book composed largely of blank pages, which Repton would have filled had he got the job.

Today the Red Books give the impression of wider landscape achievements than were ever realised. The earliest surviving Red Book is the 1789 commentary for Brandsbury in Middlesex, Repton's third commission, produced for Lady Salusbury. Over twenty years later, Repton wrote that his final publication, *Fragments on the Theory and Practice of Landscape Gardening*, drew on material from 'more than four hundred different reports in MS'. In reality he did not produce 400 Red Books, as often his recommendations took the form of letters or a sequence of sketches. Repton's obituary in *The Gentleman's Magazine* of April 1818 thus stated that he left '300 MS collections on various subjects, accompanied by drawings to explain the improvements suggested by him'.

André Rogger, in his authoritative *Landscapes of Taste: The Art of Humphry Repton's Red Books*, estimates an upper limit of 200 to 220 completed Red Books, with 123 extant and accounted for. Rogger has traced sixty-two of these existing books to their original estates, or at the very least to the clients' descendants, with forty-six preserved in British or North American

Philip John Miles, Bristol's first millionaire citizen, commissioned Repton to landscape the grounds of Leigh Court in such a way as to block out views of his neighbour's house – an 'obtrusive yellow mass of Ugliness'. Repton suggested planting three acacias on the terrace to hide the 'upstart mansion'.

The trellised arbour built over the weir at Stoneleigh Abbey probably dates from Repton's improvements for Thomas Leigh. If so, it is a rare example of a realised design, with the majority of Repton's ideas existing only as plans in his Red Books.

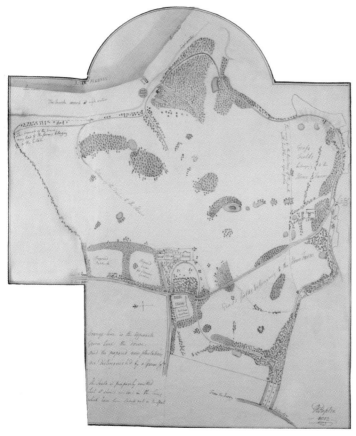

Repton's map of the estate around Hooton Hall did not fit into his standard Red Book format. Two rectangular extension flaps were needed as well as a semi-circular top flap to accommodate a bend of the Mersey.

21

libraries or archives. The remaining books are held in private collections worldwide, testament to their continued status as valuable artefacts, apart from the actual landscapes they inspired.

Jealous of the artistic vibrancy and resourcefulness of the Red Books, Repton's contemporaries frequently demeaned them as sales gimmicks. The poet and gardener William Mason, of whom Repton was an avid supporter, described how Repton 'alters places on Paper and makes them so picturesque that fine folks think that all the oaks etc. he draws … will grow exactly in the shape and fashion in which he delineated them, so they employ him at a great Price'. The Scottish botanist, author and garden designer John Claudius Loudon reckoned they demonstrated Repton's 'tinsel kind of talent' and his old friend William Marshall wrote in the *Monthly Review* in January 1796 that they turned 'rural improvement' into 'rural pantomime'.

However, Repton's patrons were not as cynical. Sir Walter Scott enjoyed the text-and-image concept precisely because it was 'a raree show omitting only the magnifying glass & substituting his red book for the box and strings'.

Repton animated many of his Red Book scenes with both workers and owners. Here women sweep the grounds of Stoneleigh Abbey's gatehouse under the watchful eye of a warder.

Having read Girardin's *De la composition des paysages* of 1777, Repton believed firmly in the French landscape theorist's maxim that no scene in nature should be attempted without first being painted. For Repton, illusionism was not a crime; it was a necessity, enabling landscape gardening to hold its own within 'the polite arts'. In his 1792 Red Book for Tatton Park, he deployed Burke's dictum, from *A Philosophical Enquiry into the Origin of Our Ideas of the Sublime and Beautiful* of 1757, that 'a true artist should put a generous deceit on spectators'. He wrote, 'We [the landscape gardener] plant a hill, to make it appear higher than it is; we open the banks of a brook to give it the appearance of a river.' If sleight-of-hand was necessary to score a commission – such as the introduction of a loitering tramp into a largely inoffensive landscape, or the exaggerated wildness of an overgrown copse – then so be it. Artistic licence could be justified:

> The imagination [is not] so fastidious as to take offence at any well supported deception, even after the want of reality is discovered. When we are interested at a tragedy, we do not enquire whence the characters are copied: on the contrary, we forget that when we see a Garrick or a Siddons, and join in the sorrows of a Belvidere or a Beverley.

For Repton, the animation of the landscape by human activity was an essential element of his designs. His Red Book illustrations were peppered with animals, happy labourers, carriages and gentlefolk, believing as he did that a '*cheerful lawn*, fed by cattle' was immeasurably superior to a '*melancholy lawn*, kept by the roller and scythe'.

Repton himself experienced difficult relationships in his professional life but he recognised the value of human interaction. He described life in Hare Street as a 'constant moving scene', which he 'would not exchange for any of the lonely parks that I have improved for others'.

Repton had immense confidence in his own abilities and saw himself as 'gifted with the peculiar faculty of seeing almost immediately the way in which [a place] might be improved', in other words, as the natural descendant to Brown, the man able to recognise an estate's 'capabilities' after only a brief circuit on horseback. His Red Books were the means by which he communicated this talent, 'delivering my reports in writing, accompanied with maps … and sketches'. The books followed a standard format, comprising a flattering dedication and general sections listed under the 'Situation' and 'Character' of the country estate, the 'Approach' to the house and 'Views from the House', before closing with specific questions about the surroundings, including 'Pleasure-ground', 'Walks', 'Water' and 'Plantations'. His language

The before-and-after sketches of Rode Hall (Cheshire) were 'most respectfully inscribed to Mrs Bootle'. Repton hoped to appeal to her feminine sensibilities by replacing an agricultural landscape with these genteel vistas.

was always flattering, sycophantic and cloying, designed to seduce clients into buying into his vision for their landscapes. Depending on the size and importance of the commission, detailed theoretical passages on aesthetics and style such as the Picturesque and Gothic were also included, interspersed with passages from Mason's lengthy, three-volume poem, *The English Garden*.

If possible, Repton included in his Red Books personal references to his visit, reinforcing – or perhaps forcing – a connection with the estate's owners. Whereas Brown had paid but fleeting visits to his employers, Repton hung around embarrassingly, desperate for acceptance.

The Babworth Red Book, completed in 1792, includes a congratulatory illustration of himself and his patrons, Mr and Mrs Simpson, forming a musical trio under an oak tree. They epitomise the very essence of gentlemanly sociability and polite conduct. To be treated as a social equal was worth more to Repton than financial reward. In 1799, when he was permitted to dine and relax each evening with the family at Harewood, he was in his element.

Employers and friends held the key both to Repton's success and to his personal happiness. He craved a social intimacy with his clients which bordered on obsequiousness, and for him landscape gardening would always be a means to an end; a way to elevate his own position in society. 'The chief benefit I have derived from it,' he wrote of his chosen profession, 'has

been the society of those to whose notice I could not otherwise have aspired.' At Hare Street, he boasted of the part he had played in reconciling the Benyon family at Gidea Hall with the Wallingers of Hare Hall. 'Two *Halls* or great houses, like two suns, cannot well exist on the same spot – a cloud of jealousy

Dullingham's lawns are infused with all the spirit of the Red Books, although Repton himself dismissed Colonel Jeafresson's site as 'attended with difficulties' following a disagreement with the Cambridgeshire landowner.

Repton immortalised himself in many of his Red Books. Here he is shown immaculately dressed in a blue topcoat, directing the expansion of the river at Stoneleigh Abbey.

25

At Dullingham House in Cambridgeshire, Repton opened out the front lawn, once walled off from the village street. A Red Book was delivered in 1802, after arguments with his patron hampered its production.

engendered by rival wealth or adjoining property, is apt to darken the sunshine of social intercourse,' he fawned.

Not all of Repton's patrons were as accommodating as Mr Simpson or Baron Harewood. The Duke of Bedford informed him bluntly that he was not called to Woburn Abbey at his leisure, neither was his opinion sought on anything beyond gardening; rather, he was charged 'to freely give me your opinion, as to what alterations or improvements suggest themselves to your judgment, leaving the execution of them to my own direction'. This was a crushing blow for the grovelling Repton.

PICTURESQUE PRESSURES

R EPTON'S EARLIEST LANDSCAPES were, unsurprisingly, scaled-down Brownian parks, designed firmly in the style of his predecessor. Storm clouds were gathering, however, in the form of the Picturesque aesthetes, who railed against these identically manicured prospects. The Brownian park was perceived to be a violation of taste by the Reverend William Gilpin (1724–1804), pioneer of the Picturesque Tour, and Repton's former friends, two Herefordshire landowners, Sir Uvedale Price and Richard Payne Knight. Savage debate ensued, the result of which was an all-out stylistic war from which the men's relationships would never recover.

By consciously styling himself England's next natural landscapist, Repton invited criticism and was reviled in print. Attacks rained down in the form of Gilpin's 1782 *Observations on the River Wye and Several Parts of South Wales*, Payne Knight's *The Landscape, a Didactic Poem* and Price's polemic, *An Essay on the Picturesque*. These last were published in 1794, sparking what became known as the Picturesque Controversy.

It did not help that Repton amassed numerous commissions in the Golden Vale of Hereford, birthplace of the Picturesque aesthetic and, in

Payne Knight laid out a Picturesque circuit around the Teme Gorge in the valley below Downton Castle. He delighted in rough vegetation, ruined buildings and melancholic sensibility, and hated Brown with a passion.

Repton's own words, 'the enemy's quarters'. But what *was* the Picturesque? Fundamentally, it was an aesthetic ideal, a literary reaction to Brown's landscape legacy. Although even Gilpin, Price and Payne Knight never fully agreed on what constituted the Picturesque model, all three mourned the diversity of the lost Rococo garden, ruthlessly levelled by the landscape park. Price lamented, 'Verdure and smoothness, which are the characteristic beauties of a lawn, are in their nature allied to monotony.' Instead they promoted an instinctual reaction to natural scenery, cliffs and cascades, and a Romantic appreciation of rugged topography. The great care Brown had taken to conceal any such roughness was disparaged by Gilpin, who wrote:

> How flat, and insipid is often the garden scene, how puerile, how absurd!
> The banks of the river, how smooth, and parallel! The lawn, and its
> boundaries, how unlike nature!

In addition, they believed that landscape design should adhere to the basic principles of Italian landscape painting in its structure, and an endless vista of grass provided no defined foreground, middle ground or distance.

Ironically, relationships between the men started off amicably enough, and the Picturesque theorists believed they had found in Repton a new recruit. Their paths first crossed in 1789 when Repton was given a new commission at Ferney Hall in Shropshire. The estate was near to Payne Knight's Downton Castle, and Repton, perhaps sensing danger, dutifully sought Payne Knight's advice on how to tackle Ferney. He even took a boat

The view from Garnons towards the Black Mountains, as Repton envisaged it at the time of his design, is a pastoral scene worthy of Brown.

Repton's 'before' depiction of Roundway in Wiltshire, from his 1794 Red Book for James Sutton.

tour with Price, who later recalled, 'I shall always remember with pleasure the hours we spent together on the Wye, and the perfect good-humour and cheerfulness of the whole party.' Payne Knight, however, was immune to flattery. He disliked Repton personally, perceiving him to be a social climber, but believed, together with Price, that he might be persuaded into embracing the Picturesque ethos and fashioned into one of their own. As an emergent landscape gardener desperate for acceptance, Repton presented a much smaller threat than the unshakeable Brown. Accordingly, when Price wrote to Lord Abercorn of their new acquaintance he was optimistic:

> I have lately had an opportunity of seeing a good deal of Mr Repton, a layer-
> out of grounds, or as he styles himself a Landscape Gardener: you will guess

Repton's ideas for improvements at Roundway were textbook Brown, with serpentine water, open pasture and the tree clumps so despised by Price.

at his manners by his title which I believe is of his own creation, but tho a coxcomb he is very ingenious in his profession, & seems to me to have infinitely more resources, & better principles, than his predecessors: Knight is acquainted with him, & thinks about him as I do, & we both rejoice that he has some respect for picturesque beauty which has hitherto been treated with great indignity. He has been making plans of improvement for some Gentlemen in my neighbourhood at whose houses I saw him, & afterwards went down the Wye with him, & was happy to find that he really admired the banks in their natural state.

This fragile state of cordiality was lost forever when Repton made clear his intentions as Brown's successor. In Price's words, he took 'the opposite side … a circumstance which is sincerely lamented by many of your friends and well-wishers'. The two men quickly closed ranks against Repton, Payne Knight thereafter dismissing his schemes as 'designed and executed exactly after Mr Brown's receipt, without any attention to the natural or artificial character of a place'. Seemingly unconcerned with this simmering animosity, Repton clung to the belief that he was Brown's inheritor and laid out his earliest commissions proudly in the style of a landscape park, replete with serpentine waters, bald lawns and clumps of trees, ignoring Price's appeal to stand on his own merits.

Unperturbed by his failed overtures at Ferney, Repton boldly carried out improvements along Brownian lines both at Bulstrode in Buckinghamshire and for Peter Burrell at Langley, in Kent, the following year. Both these pleasure grounds were formulaic, laced with sinuous paths and a shrubbery

At Tatton Park, Repton gentrified the approach from Knutsford by rebuilding 'a few miserable cottages' and erecting a gate lodge with triumphal arch. This would create 'the first essential Greatness in a place', and unite the park with the town.

near the house, similar to those laid out by Brown at Trentham in Staffordshire in 1759. Regrettably, much to the chagrin of the upwardly mobile Repton, working predominantly for the aristocracy, as Brown had done, was no longer possible. Indeed, during the 1780s and 1790s large numbers of minor squires and middling merchants were looking to improve their standing in society with a fashionably landscaped park, and Repton was not so proud as to turn away work. Rather, he developed the idea of 'appropriation', or the ability to visibly confer consequence upon an estate. This technique enabled Repton to adapt his early landscapes to the needs and social status of his patrons. He was obsessed with the notion that a landscape reflected the prestige of its owner. The Red Book he produced for William Egerton at Tatton Park in 1792 explained:

> The first essential of greatness in a place, is the appearance of united and uninterrupted property ... There are various ways by which this effect

Marked with a 'C' on the Red Book map for Garnons is the serpentine water which would 'shew an apparent continuation' of the River Wye. This piece of visual trickery survives.

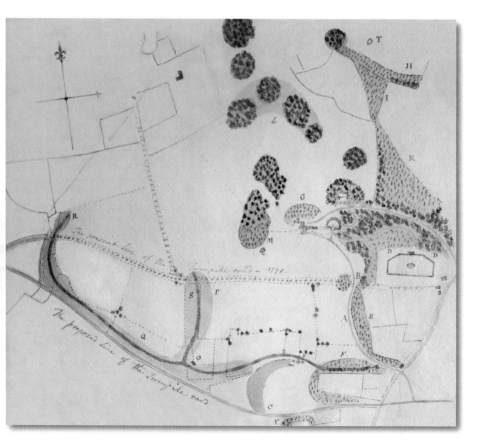

is occasionally produced ... viz. the church, and churchyards, may be decorated in a style that shall in some degree correspond with that of the mansion; – the market-house, or other public edifice, an obelisk, or even a *mere* stone, with distances, may be made an ornament to the town, and bear the arms of the family.

Naturally the Picturesque writers disagreed, Price stating: 'There is no such enemy to the real improvement of the beauty of grounds as the foolish vanity of making a parade of their extent.'

Repton's obsession with status was the driving force behind his first Herefordshire commission at Garnons in 1791 for John Geers Cotterell. The Red Book dripped with the sugary sentiments in which Repton excelled:

The Character of a place will take its distinguishing marks from the united consideration of its situation and the extent of territory surrounding. Both these at Garnons require a degree of Greatness which neither the house nor the Grounds at present indicate.

Brown's influence on Repton is evident in the harmonious landscaping around Garnons House, which Repton worked on with William Wilkins.

The house was, Repton continued, 'the seat of Hospitality and, where according to the custom of Herefordshire, not only the neighbouring Families but even their servants and horses may receive a welcome'. Cotterell's estate lay perilously close to Price's secluded home at Foxley, but even this did not dissuade Repton from adopting a Brownian approach to the improvements.

All surrounding arable fields were to be enclosed and incorporated into the pasture land, a lake was to be dug at the foot of the hill and clumps of trees were planted either side of a serpentine drive to cloak the steep hillside. With a surreptitious dig at the Picturesque theorists, the Garnons Red Book even noted that 'the more wild and romantic continuation of the drive over the hills at the back of the house' would be used less than the smooth main approach, because there would be 'difficulty in removing all ideas of danger from the pleasure which such a drive would excite'. So Repton's early parks were, like Brown's, intended to encourage leisurely sporting pursuits and the quiet contemplation of nature, rather than the stimulations and thrills craved by advocates of the Picturesque such as Payne Knight and Price.

Price was a conservationist, and as such his interpretation of the Picturesque was an appreciation of unadorned nature: craggy rocks, mossy pools and fern-darkened ditches. He was much keener on Picturesque theory than practical landscaping, and his own wooded valleys at Foxley were abandoned to grow wild around the forlorn Gothick garden buildings laid out by his father and grandfather. When galvanised by his ally and neighbour Payne Knight to publish his *Essay*, Price castigated the natural landscapist, and therefore by implication Repton, for the practice of smoothing and levelling the ground, writing:

> The moment this mechanical common place operation (by which Mr Brown and his followers have gained so much credit) is begun, adieu to all that the painter admires – to all intricacies – to all the beautiful varieties of form, tint, light and shade, every deep recess – every bold projection – the fantastic root of trees – the winding paths of sheep – all must go; in a few hours the rash hand of false taste completely demolishes what time only, and a thousand lucky incidents, can mature.

In addition, Price criticised the Brownian tree clump, 'whose name, if the first letter was taken away, would most accurately describe its form and effect'. The guardians of the Picturesque equated smoothness with monotony, promoting instead the 'accident and neglect' of landscapes such as Foxley's.

The pressure exerted upon Repton by his former friends to defect from the Brownian school of landscaping was immense. A month before Price's devastating publication, Payne Knight's poem *The Landscape* had glorified the virtues of a Picturesque scene. He was no kinder to Brown, accusing him of 'Spreading o'er its unprolific spawn / in never-ending sheets of vapid lawn.' In addition, its famous illustrations by Thomas Hearne drove the point home cruelly. A dull classical house, frivolous Chinese bridge and perfectly manicured Brownian layout was contrasted with an overgrown Picturesque

Following page: Garnons after Repton's improvements was enriched with all the features of a Brownian landscape: sweeping lawns, clumps of trees, curving sheets of water and peacefully grazing sheep.

composition of rugged rocks, alpine bridge and rambling Elizabethan house. Unlike Gilpin and Price, Payne Knight practiced what he preached. At Downton Castle, he exploited all the gloomy potential of a house sited on a rocky gorge, with a perilous circuit walk littered with Picturesque incidents and rickety bridges.

Despite these criticisms of the Brownian approach, Repton believed all was going well with his new profession. Since his first commission at Catton, he had had a steady stream of contracts, including a trio of prestigious gardens in Nottinghamshire: Welbeck Abbey for the Duke of Portland in 1789, Anthony Eyre's Grove Hall in 1790 and Thoresby Hall the following year for Charles Pierrepont. Unfortunately, with Price living next door to the new landscape park he had designed for Garnons, Repton was never going to sneak below the radar for long.

Sure enough, following the twin attacks on Brown's minimalist aesthetic in 1794, the spotlight shifted directly onto an unsuspecting Repton. Taken aback by the personal nature of the attacks from men he had once counted as friends, Repton stood firm in his convictions. In his 1795 Red Book for Sufton Court, also in Herefordshire, he defended himself by taking the moral high ground:

> I have little leisure to enter the lists with Mr Price or Mr Knight, and must therefore decline a public controversy which in the hands of the latter gentlemen is becoming indecently personal.

Payne Knight's circuit walk at Downton Castle included this gloomy Cold Bath, or 'Sulky' as he termed it. William Owen's painting shows him enjoying a book there in splendid Romantic isolation.

After such a successful start, Repton could not resist an opportunity to boast: 'It is however no small circumstance of triumph to me, that I am still consulted *even in the enemy's quarters*; and for that good opinion of my professional skill.'

Certainly, Herefordshire commissions poured in, much to the consternation of Price and Payne Knight. Work for Cotterell at Garnons had been superseded by that at Stoke Edith in 1792 for Edward Foley, followed almost immediately by a commission at Moccas Court for Sir George Cornewall and that at Sufton for James Hereford. Neither was Repton alone in his belief that the landscape park continued to be the embodiment of true taste: he had an ally in the form of John Matthews, owner of Belmont, yet another estate in the vale sited upriver from Moccas Court. Repton was working for Matthews around the time the latter anonymously published the poem *A Sketch from the Landscape* in 1794. In it, Matthews defended Brown and Repton against what he termed the 'unnatural extravagances' of 'these desperate

With the flap in place, Repton emphasised the artificial nature of the existing rectangular water feature at Garnons.

Once the flap is lifted, the prospect at Garnons is transformed. A carriage drive and bridge span Repton's new curved piece of water, deceiving the visitor 'to suppose he sees a stretch of the Wye, which he knows must flow at no great distance'.

Here John Matthews parodies Payne Knight's *The Worship of Priapus*, depicting two young women swooning in the face of Pan, the god of gardens, with his 'huge and terrible *Priapus*'.

amateurs'. The title page depicted these 'amateurs' hurling the contents of a chamber pot at a monument to Brown, while the end page presented a picture of Payne Knight as a sex-obsessed dilettante.

Backed up by the public approbation of such patrons, Repton's Red Book for Sufton began:

> My opinion concerning the improvement of Sufton Court involves so many points, which I deem principles in the Art of Landscape Gardening, that I trust you will permit me to take this opportunity of justifying my practice, in opposition to the wild theory of the improvement which has lately sprung up in Herefordshire.

In contrast to this grand opening, Repton's work for James Hereford was disappointingly minimal, perhaps because his visit was 'made in two days of excessive rainy weather', with 'no assistance from previous knowledge of the spot, or from any accurate survey of the premises'. Existing plantations crowded and obscured the house, cutting it off from

John Matthews caricatured the criticism of Brown in this engraving, made eleven years after his death. The contents of a chamber pot are hurled unceremoniously at a monument to Brown's memory.

Repton's 'before' sketch for Brandsbury (Middlesex), reproduced by John Claudius Loudon.

the rest of the landscape park. Thus Repton concentrated on pruning and thinning these trees to reveal open pasture, while retaining a few artfully placed clumps to frame the view.

The end result was another typically Brownian park, complete with serpentine carriage drives and boundless lawns. Defiantly, Repton noted his improvements were the result of 'the axe rather than the spade', as the Picturesque approach to landscape was 'to plant largely and cut down sparingly'. Such conservationist views were, Repton wrote, merely the 'over cautious advice of a timorous inexperience'. The gloves were well and truly off.

Repton's 'after' sketch for Brandsbury, showing similar improvements to those carried out for James Hereford at Sufton Court. Repton replaced a pale fence with a sunken ha-ha to open up the landscape scene.

THEORY AND PRACTICE

A FERVENT BELIEF in the value of landscape aesthetics underpinned all Repton's projects, particularly following the Picturesque Controversy of 1794. 'I have made it a general practice to deliver my opinion in writing,' he said; subsequently, many of his Red Books defended his work.

Over the course of his life Repton published several volumes on garden design: *Sketches and Hints on Landscape Gardening* (1794), *Observations on the Theory and Practice of Landscape Gardening* (1803), *An Inquiry into the Changes in Taste in Landscape Gardening* (1806) and *Fragments on the Theory and Practice of Landscape Gardening* (1816).

These writings engaged with contemporary fashion and enabled Repton to circulate his ideas and fully exploit his market. By fusing contemporary passions for travel writing, topographical drawing and amateur art appreciation within the prevailing rhetoric of taste, Repton elevated the standing of the landscape gardener.

Taste was a theoretical concept so widely discussed during the eighteenth century that the social commentator George Coleman condemned it as being 'the great fashion of our time', writing:

> Taste is at present the darling idol of the polite world ... The fine ladies and gentlemen dress with Taste; the architects, whether Gothic or Chinese, build with Taste; the painters paint with Taste; critics read with Taste; and in short, fiddlers, players, singers, dancers, and mechanics themselves, are all the sons and daughters of Taste. Yet in this amazing super-abundance of Taste, few can say what it really is, or what the word itself signifies.

Taste formed the leitmotif of Horace Walpole's essay *The History of the Modern Taste in Gardening*; the acquisition of taste was the driving force behind the Continental Grand Tour and innumerable manuals and journals were published, all dedicated to the art of gentlemanly behaviour. For Repton, it was 'the business of Taste to deceive ... by which Art endeavours to

Opposite:
The suggested rotunda for Leigh Court was to have been sited on a knoll, providing views of two Gothic towers on the horizon: Cook's Folly and Blaise Castle.

This tableau was included with Repton's designs for Brighton Pavilion. It displayed his maxim, inspired by Burke, that 'Gardens are works of art rather than of nature'.

A colour wheel, reproduced by Loudon in 1840, illustrates Repton's theories on colour mixing. He believed this was 'not the effect of chance or fancy but guided by certain general laws of nature'.

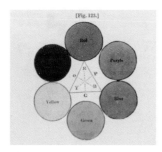

conceal her own works, and make them appear the products of Nature only'. Reconciling his skills as a salesman with his position as a man of taste enabled him to place landscape gardening at the heart of Georgian culture.

The pursuit of taste might have been constant but Repton's ideologies were slowly wavering. Through his writings he duly forged a new style, paradoxically drawing on Picturesque principles. Repton had, of course, praised scenery of the kind admired by Gilpin from an early stage in his career, professing 'that he sought the principles of his art, not in the works of Kent or Brown, but in those of the great landscape painters'.

Probably his most successfully realised Red Book design achieved a satisfying balance between the ideal parkscapes of Brown and his imitators, and a Picturesque wilderness. This was his 1795 scheme for the Quaker banker John Scandrett Harford, owner of the Blaise Castle estate, four miles south of Bristol. Spread out behind Harford's new house was a dramatically hilly landscape carved by a deep ravine, gloomy enough to satisfy even Payne

The Red Book overlays proved so popular that Repton reproduced them within three sumptuous volumes when business was flagging. Here is an example from *Observations*, published in 1803.

Knight's brooding melancholy. Here Repton laid out perilously winding carriage drives around a series of contrived views. The Lover's Leap, the Precipice, a Woodsman's Cottage and a Sham Castle all provided a sharp contrast to the gentle greensward surrounding the house.

Softened to the preferences of his enemies, when Repton came to design the landscape at Sheringham Park in 1812 he 'was infinitely pleased' with the Upchers' 'romantic scenery and bold swells crowned with woods'. Written with all the fervour of the newly converted, his Red Book proposed the preservation of this 'accidental character' of imperfectly forested slopes and a break away from the usual 'dull, vapid, smooth and tranquil scene'. This last was a direct quotation from Payne Knight's *The Landscape*, and as such a slap in the face of Brown's memory. It was not just Repton that regretted the loss of former camaraderie with the Picturesque aesthetes, however, as Price wrote to him in 1810:

Repton's theoretic principles encouraged an appreciation of landscape aesthetics. This plate demonstrates the effect of 'perpendicular' Gothic architecture and 'spiry topped' trees.

The Red Book plan for nearby Leigh Court marks radiating viewpoints, including 'Oblique View towards Blaize [sic] Castle Tower'. Obscuring the 'large staring yellow house' opposite, belonging to rival banker Edward Protheroe, caused Repton serious trouble.

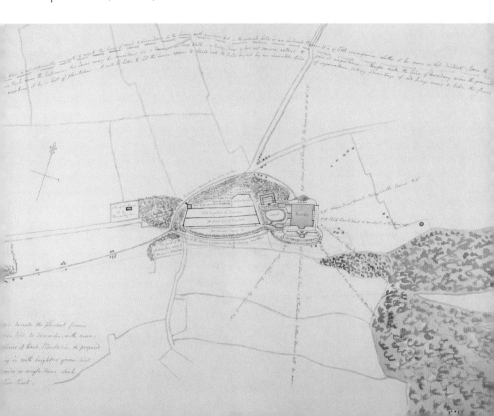

Repton's great fondness for Sheringham Hall (Norfolk) stemmed from his having lived in the nearby village of Sustead for twelve years.

From the time I had first the pleasure of being acquainted with you, I wished to be your ally, not your opponent: I flattered myself, that, having considered the same subject in different lights, and by means of a different course of study, we might have been of reciprocal use to each other. I felt great hopes that you might employ your talents (which I thought would naturally lead you in that way) in making experiments in landscape-gardening on the principles of landscape-painting, and in the art of painting in general.

Backpedalling from his initial stance as successor to Brown, Repton wrote in his *Observations*:

> Where a rattling turbulent mountain-stream passes through a rocky valley, like the Derwent at Chatsworth, perhaps Mr Brown was wrong in checking its noisy course, to produce the glassy surface of a slow moving river.

After years of opposing the Picturesque theorists and enduring their harsh criticism, Repton began to adopt their ways of thinking. He wrote:

This sweeping coastal view created at Sheringham in Norfolk survives as part of Repton's best-preserved and favourite landscape.

When I compare the picturesque scenery of Downton Vale with the meagre efforts of art which are attributed to the school of Brown, I cannot wonder at the enthusiastic abhorrence which the author of *The Landscape* expresses for modern gardening.

The combined impact of the bullying he had suffered and the realisation that he actually found varied landscapes appealing led Repton to abandon his earlier principles. Even on that first placatory visit to Downton he had been forced to agree that it was 'enriched by caves and cells, hovels and covered seats, or other buildings, in perfect harmony with the wild but pleasing horrors of the scene'. Repton was, perhaps, the embodiment of that cliché: 'he who tries to please everybody pleases nobody'. He attempted, unsuccessfully, to toe the line between the natural landscapists of the Brownian school and the emerging disciples of the Picturesque, and in so doing tied himself up in knots.

Repton's rejection of the Brownian aesthetic was significantly sweetened by a shift in demand from his patrons, who were now urging diversity, but were

unsure how to accommodate the dramatic gorges of the Picturesque within their more modest estates. Even Payne Knight was growing tired of gloom and savagery and built himself Stonebrook Cottage, a modest, cosy retreat down the road from Downton. Finally, it was not much of a leap between the wilder natural scenery admired by Gilpin and Price, to the tamer, more commercialised Picturesque that Repton adopted at Blaise Castle or Holkham Hall, with their 'snug thatched cottage[s], picturesquely embosomed in the trees'. Both styles reacted to the formulaic simplicity of the landscape park with more varied surfaces and interesting detail, and celebrated man-made as well as natural features in the tradition of the Rococo circuit. A taste for rugged rather than smooth nature, Edmund Burke's sublime rather than the beautiful, had supplanted the Brownian aesthetic, and Repton began to reassess his predecessor's achievements.

Throughout his career Repton attempted, unsuccessfully, to reconcile the two opposing styles of architecture prevalent at the end of the century: Gothic and Grecian.

THE GARDENESQUE

Continuing to condemn ideas he had once embraced, Repton concluded in 1816 that the tradition of 'surrounding a house by a naked grass field' was a 'bald and insipid custom, introduced by Brown'. With that, he turned his back forever on the manicured park.

The development of the eighteenth-century landscape garden was, then, a series of actions and reactions: Brown's generation of natural landscapists reacting to the earlier artificial Arcadian layouts, and now Repton and the Picturesque writers rejecting Brown's minimalism. However, Repton's intentions were first and foremost to please his clients. Obsessed with status and genteel hospitality, his aims were always to cater for social convenience over and above ideological consistency. He condemned the oppression of the poorer classes while revelling in the company of the comfortably rich. He derided stylistic eclecticism and then combined Hindu, Muslim and Chinese influences to spectacular effect within his designs for Brighton Pavilion.

Repton had become receptive to Picturesque ideas, yet in 1795, dismissed the 'scenes of horror' lauded by the Picturesque tourist as fit only for 'the representations of a pencil'. Now he was free to come up with the compromise that would capitalise on a changing society, and make his name.

This was the emergent Gardenesque, a fussy, bourgeois style that Repton perfected for his newest clientele. These families were not blessed with the ancient woodlands and infinite lawns of Brown's aristocratic estates, and even those that were – such as the Hardwickes of Wimpole Hall – had been blinded to the charms of a pastoral landscape by the dramatic picturesque vistas they had seen on their travels. At home they craved comfort and novelty, and Repton's designs, by skilfully linking the house to the garden via a rosary, trellised walkway or terrace, provided both.

Through the Gardenesque, the affected and impressionable Repton at last achieved his own true style, anticipating Victorian sensibilities and advocating a return to formality. Indeed, it was John Claudius Loudon

Opposite: Capability Brown might have 'shared the private hours of the King' but Repton hung about on the periphery of the Royal Family. Faced with this extravagant proposal for Brighton Pavilion, Mrs. Fitzherbert remarked only: 'And pray what is all this to cost?'

The Italianate style of balustraded terraces, which characterised Repton's Gardenesque, phased quite naturally into the split-level shrubbery walks of the Victorian pleasure ground.

who brought the term 'Gardenesque' into common usage in the nineteenth century, although many of Repton's later designs for landscapes such as at Stoneleigh Abbey and Endsleigh perfectly encapsulated the style's features and botanical variety. Writing in the *Gardener's Magazine* in December 1832, Loudon argued:

Mere picturesque improvement is not enough in these enlightened times: it is necessary to understand that there is such a character of art as the gardenesque, as well as the picturesque. The very term gardenesque, perhaps, will startle some readers; but we are convinced, nevertheless, that it is a term which will soon find a place in the language of rural art.

As always, a practical force was at work behind this latest aesthetic shift. The turn of the century forced Repton to respond to a changing economic scene, as an increasingly urbanised Britain traded its agricultural base for an industrial heart of factories and manufacturing progress. A rising middle class of businessmen and industrialists threatened to overwhelm the nobility, and Repton was there waiting, ready to steer their landscaping needs in a lucrative direction. Writing in 1816, he acknowledged the extent to which the social and economic climate of the Industrial Revolution influenced his later designs:

Gardenesque improvements for Sir William Stanley's Hooton included viewing balconies, a pergola with blossoming climbers and a formal wall decorated with urns. Repton was more than usually patronising to his young client.

It seldom falls to the lot of the improver to be called upon for his opinion on places of great extent ... while in the neighbourhood of every city or manufacturing town, new places as villas are daily springing up, and these, with a few acres, require all the conveniences, comforts, appendages, of larger and more sumptuous, if not more expensive places. And ... these have of late had the greatest claim to my attention.

In terms of the Gardenesque, booming industrialisation led to advances in greenhouse technology, allowing exotic plants to be reared more easily, and encouraging interconnections between drawing rooms and conservatories, and interior and exterior spaces.

Repton was also motivated by sheer common sense. The modest suburban villa could not possibly accommodate Picturesque mountain scenery half as easily as his new concept of an adaptable garden on a human scale. What Repton did was to place mounting emphasis on just one element of the Picturesque landscape: the foreground, or area immediately surrounding the house. Working within these more confined spheres encouraged greater attention to detail, instigating a necessary preference for flower gardens over never-ending swathes of lawn and lengthy belts of woodland. In such a way, Gardenesque layouts, with their pleasure grounds immediately surrounding the house, bridged the gap between the boundless parks of the landed classes and the compact villa gardens of the Victorian and Edwardian eras. The self-made industrialist wanted for everyday convenience, comfortable garden rooms and all-weather conservatories.

Tom Williamson concludes in *Polite Landscapes: Gardens and Society in Eighteenth-Century England* that it was not, as with the established estates of the landed classes, by 'adding field to field, or by taking away hedges, or

Brighton Pavilion's sprawling complex of hothouses enabled the royal gardeners to grow and display exotic plant specimens, even in the depths of winter.

by removing roads to a distance' that a villa's environs were enhanced. Rather Repton improved his customers' properties by exploiting 'every circumstance of interest or beauty within our reach, and by hiding such objects as cannot be viewed with pleasure'.

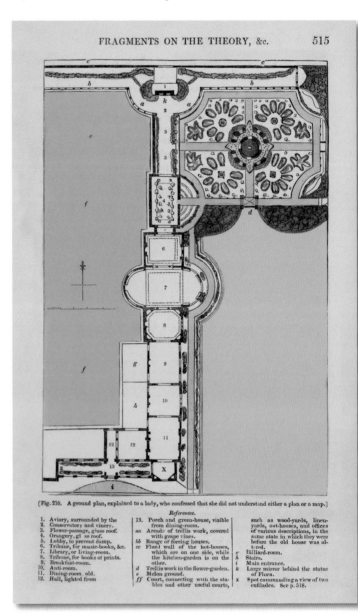

FRAGMENTS ON THE THEORY, &c.   515

[Fig. 210. A ground plan, explained to a lady, who confessed that she did not understand either a plan or a map.]

References.

1. Aviary, surrounded by the
2. Conservatory and vinery.
3. Flower-passage, glass roof.
4. Orangery, gl ss roof.
5. Lobby, to prevent damp.
6. Tribune, for music-books, &c.
7. Library, or living-room.
8. Tribune, for books of prints.
9. Breakfast-room.
10. Anti-room.
11. Dining-room old.
12. Hall, lighted from

13. Porch and green-house, visible from dining-room.
aa Arcade of trellis work, covered with grape vines.
bb Range of forcing houses.
cc Flued wall of the hot-houses, which are on one side, while the kitchen-garden is on the other.
d   Trellis work in the flower-garden.
e   Melon ground.
ff Court, connecting with the stables and other useful courts,

such as wood-yards, linen-yards, out-houses, and offices of various descriptions, in the same state in which they were before the old house was al-t-red.
g   Billiard-room.
h   Stairs.
i   Main entrance.
k   Large mirror behind the statue of Flora.
x   Spot commanding a view of two enfilades. See p. 518.

In this plan, a chain of linear rooms banishes the distinction between house and garden. Repton was largely responsible for introducing the concept of garden rooms.

For the avid garden tourist, yearly excursions to the Wye Valley or Scottish Highlands provided a regular dose of Picturesque thrills, allowing Repton's customers to commission bowling-greens, flowering shrubs and safely gravelled paths closer to home. In Repton's own words:

> While mouldering abbeys and the antiquated cottage with its chimney smothered in ivy may be eminently appealing to the painter, in whatever relates to man, propriety and convenience are not less objectives of good taste than picturesque effects.

By 1804 Repton was conjuring up a complicated series of pleasure grounds for his cantankerous employer, the Duke of Bedford, at Woburn. These included an American Garden and a Chinese Garden. He wrote: 'The gardens, or pleasure-grounds, near a house, may be considered as so many

Repton's design for a Pheasantry at Brighton Pavilion was the height of exoticism. He believed Indian architecture to be both deeply ancient and highly modern, writing that 'cast iron is peculiarly adapted to some light parts of the Indian style'.

Brighton was a year-round destination, and Repton created for the pavilion 'a garden which should not be affected by any variations of season'. The design for the Chinese Garden in front of the suite of Chinese rooms next to the private apartments included wicker flower baskets ablaze with colour.

Repton's transformative vision for Endsleigh's water-side gardens included these terraced flowerbeds, a great conservatory and *treillaged* walks.

Below: Endsleigh's formal gardens running down to the River Tamar survive almost exactly as Repton envisaged them, two hundred years ago.

different apartments belonging to its state, its comfort and its pleasure.' For the Earl of Bridgewater at Ashridge, Repton designed fifteen separate gardens, including a Mount Garden, Monk's Garden and another American Garden, similar to the one laid out at Woburn nine years previously.

Vast swathes of uninterrupted lawn might have complemented the sporting lifestyles of the landed gentry, but for many of Repton's clients with their modest suburban homes, trellis-covered walkways and raised

beds of planting were far more suitable. The easy intimacy of the Rococo garden's exotic circuit walks still held much appeal, and Repton set about reintroducing formal features to landscapes starved of incident. Gardens were littered with pergolas and fountains, specimen trees were marked with metal name tags, shrubberies were threaded with gravel paths and punctuated by urns on pedestals, satisfying his clients' hunger for human interest without resorting to perilous bridges or sinister caves.

By 1816 Repton had completely reversed his opinion regarding the virtues of a barren park: 'The Pleasures of a Garden have of late been very much neglected', he wrote, because of 'the prevailing custom of placing a House in the middle of a Park, detached from all objects, whether of convenience or magnificence'. This was a custom he himself had once encouraged, of course, at estates such as Garnons and Sufton Court.

Repton's 1801 Red Book for Wimpole Hall represents the Cambridgeshire estate's final stage of extended landscape improvements, initiated by

Endsleigh's arboretum contains beautiful trees from around the world, standing in spots once marked out with bamboo canes by a holidaying Duchess of Bedford.

One of Repton's last commissions, Endsleigh incorporated all his favourite features including a thatched lodge and this picturesque dell, complete with rickety alpine bridge.

The 1801 Red
Book scheme for
re-establishing an
enclosed garden
to the north of
Wimpole Hall. The
site is a palimpsest
of garden history
through four
centuries.

Oxnead Hall's
formal gardens in
Norfolk, drawn
here by John Adey
Repton, are likely
to have influenced
his father's
parterre design
for Beaudesert in
Staffordshire.

George London and Henry Wise at the end of the seventeenth century. Repton's main concern with Wimpole, as with many of the estates he worked on towards the end of his career, was with its lack of formal garden areas.

He wrote, without a hint of embarrassment, that 'there is no part of Mr Brown's system which I have had more difficulty in correcting than the absurd fashion of bringing cattle to the windows of a house. It is called natural, but to me it has ever appeared unnatural that a palace should rise immediately out of a sheep pasture'. Repton wanted to reintroduce an enclosed garden area to the north of the Hall. He also argued for an iron railing to be inserted between the outer corners of the two wings of the house, with a central gateway leading out into the wider park. Something resembling this garden was eventually laid out around 1825 by Hardwicke's land agent, Robert Withers. However, Lady Elizabeth Hardwicke quashed Repton's idea for a wall of railings, noting firmly in the margin of the Red Book that: 'This would cost too much money – and the effect doubtful.' Unlike with Brown's parklands, Repton's Gardenesque did not have economic viability to recommend it.

Repton's plans for Wimpole illustrate perfectly the purpose of the early Gardenesque style, which was the re-establishment of the garden proper, with all its neglected formal features and traditional compartmentalised plantings. In Repton's own words, 'Close clipp'd box, th' embroider'd bed / In rows and formal order laid.' Patrons demanded again the geometric parterres of the early formal garden; the Earl of Uxbridge at Beaudesert,

Staffordshire, requiring Repton to provide such a feature to update his empty landscape park.

Repton was not alone in encouraging this return to formality. In 1808, the writer and furniture designer Thomas Hope actively promoted the reintroduction of formal gardens to the immediate environs of his own garden at the Deepdene in Surrey, which was divided by stepped terraces and balustrades and crowded with urns, sculpture and alcoves. Similarly, by 1810 prominent designers such as Lewis Kennedy were busy designing extensive parterres for country houses, such as the Italian Garden at Chiswick House, Middlesex.

The Picturesque aesthetic had successfully revived the intellectual associations between painting and landscape that had lain dormant since the classical Arcadias of the 1720s and 1730s. When combined with the Gardenesque, the two styles succeeded in challenging the absolute power of the landscape park in favour of variety and designed incidents.

According to Loudon, 'This change in taste shows a real advance in intellectual enjoyment; because it carries with it the associations connected with genera and species, in addition to those of form, colour and combination.' Smooth lawns enhanced the classically proportioned houses of the previous century, but increasingly elaborate manor houses and irregularly designed suburban villas needed a suitably structured garden to underpin their asymmetry. For Beaudesert, Repton suggested the following:

> The venerable dignity of this place is not to be measured by the scale of a villa, or the spruce modern seat of sudden affluence, *be-belted* and *be-clumped* in the newest style of the modern taste of Landscape Gardening – No – rather let us go back to former times, when the lofty terrace of the *privy garden* gave protection and seclusion to the noble persons.

The 'before' sketch of Beaudesert in Repton's Red Book of 1813 reveals a humble agricultural landscape (see also overleaf).

Repton's 1816 *Fragments*, dubbed his 'stylistic will and last testament' by Timothy Mowl, is one long, florid argument in favour of the Gardenesque. Echoing Hearne's iconic illustrations for Payne Knight's *The Landscape,* in *Fragments* Repton juxtaposed two contrasting treatments of the same property. The example chosen was the White Lodge in Richmond Park, depicted first

Repton's designs for Beaudesert were too costly and grandiose to implement. They included a cascade, boating lake, Gothic dam and dramatically terraced garden.

floating rudderless on a Brownian lawn ('the uncleanly, pathless grass of a forest') and then anchored securely against a broad gravel path, flanked with *treillage* and looking triumphantly Gardenesque. Repton's commentary is characteristically saccharine: 'The Improvement has been executed in every respect by the present noble Inhabitant.' In reality, Lord Sidmouth added only the straight formal path, postponing indefinitely the '*Treillage* Ornaments' and profusion of roses. Even so, the unadorned landscape park was slowly being pushed aside, to make room for horticultural embellishment and defined garden rooms.

Alcoves and flower gardens, pathways, conservatories and Italianate stone terraces only increased in popularity as the new century advanced. Repton's gardens surrounding Leigh Court were to be in the 'more magnificent style of Italian Gardening in which Terraces & Vases & flights of Steps & Fountains' were 'blended with flowers & shrubs'.

By 1838 Loudon was writing that 'we should wish to see every lady have her flower-garden and conservatory' and 'every gentleman his arboretum, or, at all events, a gardenesque plantation of choice trees and shrubs'. As for Repton, he emerged relatively unscathed from the misunderstandings surrounding the Picturesque aesthetic, and provided an individual contribution to the history of the English landscape garden that had nothing to do with 'Capability' Brown. The expensive bourgeois clutter of a Reptonian layout was, in fact, a complete reversal of the entire Brownian aesthetic. For Repton himself, the flower garden, framing the suburban villa, was now his landscape of choice:

In SPRING the garden begins to excite interest with the first blossoms of the crocus and snowdrop: and though its delights are seldom enjoyed in the more magnificent country residences of the Nobility, yet the garden of the Villa should be profusely supplied with all the fragrance and the beauty of blossom belonging to 'il gioventu del anno'.

Francis Goodwin's pattern book, *Domestic Architecture*, was widely consulted by garden owners. His images of idealised Gardenesque layouts such as this one contributed to the dissemination of Reptonian ideas abroad.

The Gardenesque was a decisive shift in fashion, driven by industrialisation, from the serene landscape park and classically proportioned house, with its wide open spaces and glassy waters, to the more intimate villa garden, enlivened once again with shrubberies and garden incidents. Writing just before

Stoneleigh's improved landscape contained all the pleasures of the Gardenesque: a wreathed pergola set above a boathouse, latticework and island beds of roses. Wet-weather strolling was encouraged on the new loggia.

he died, Repton consigned the Brownian park, and by implication the landed rich, to history:

> A large extent of ground without moving objects, however neatly kept, is but a melancholy scene ... If solitude delights, we seek it rather in the covert of a wood, or the sequestered alcove of a flower garden, than in the open lawn.

The beginning of the eighteenth century had seen the formal garden give way to the landscape park, but by its close, the reverse was happening and the garden was blossoming again. In Repton's own words:

Frederick Sargood laid out his suburban pleasure grounds at Rippon Lea in Victoria, Australia, in the Gardenesque style. This 1880 photograph shows the compartmentalised Orange Garden, so called because of the white-flowering oranges, lemons and citrons in its outermost bed.

This Repton designed Gothic Revival garden room at Plas Newydd in Anglesey inspired Alexander Jackson Davis's 1844 hexagonal pavilion at Montgomery Place in New York.

Constantini's 1854 view of Windsor Park, Tasmania, proves the influence of the Gardenesque on the colonies, with an elaborate garden building and a pleasure ground to the rear of the *treillaged* homestead.

The house is no longer a huge pile, standing naked on a vast grazing ground: its walls are enriched with roses and jasmines; its apartments are perfumed with odours from flowers surrounding it on every side … All around is neatness, elegance, and comfort.

By the mid-nineteenth century the Gardenesque reigned unchallenged. Although the flower garden was by no means a Reptonian invention, the early Victorian layout, with its bowers, trelliswork and stone terraces, owed much to Repton's Gardenesque. His mature style had reconnected the house and the garden, with all its traditional formal features.

Notwithstanding, Humphry Repton's most important achievement was an artistic one. The text-and-image concept of the Red Book is today more widely recognised than any of his executed schemes, and it was with this ingenious sales device that he exerted a formative influence on the landscaping aesthetics of his contemporaries and beyond.

In 1840, an ailing Loudon seized upon the appeal of the Red Books, where painted landscape was transformed by the lifting of a paper flap. Finding himself sliding into debt, he republished Repton's *Sketches and Hints*, *Observations* and *Fragments*, themselves re-workings of the Red Book designs, in an inexpensive format, entitled *The Landscape Gardening and Landscape Architecture of the Late Humphry Repton, Esq.* Loudon's book introduced the Gardenesque to designers and architects as far away as America and Australia, thus ensuring that Repton's influence on the villa gardens of the nineteenth century was not only widespread but endured well beyond the landscape gardener's lifetime.

FURTHER READING

Carter, George, Goode, Patrick and Laurie, Kedrun (eds). *Humphry Repton: Landscape Gardener*. Sainsbury Centre for Visual Arts, 1982.

Daniels, Stephen. *Humphry Repton: Landscape Gardening and the Geography of Georgian England*. Yale University Press, 1999.

Loudon, John Claudius (ed). *The Landscape Gardening and Landscape Architecture of the Late Humphry Repton, Esq., Being his Entire Works on These Subjects*. Cambridge University Press, 2013.

Mowl, Timothy. *Gentlemen & Players: Gardeners of the English Landscape*. Sutton Publishing, 2000.

Mowl, Timothy and Bradney, Jane. *Historic Gardens of Herefordshire: The Historic Gardens of England*. Redcliffe Press, 2012.

Rogger, André. *Landscapes of Taste: The Art of Humphry Repton's Red Books*. Routledge, 2007.

Stroud, Dorothy. *Humphry Repton*. Country Life, 1962.

Williamson, Tom. *Polite Landscapes: Gardens and Society in Eighteenth-Century England*. Sutton Publishing, 1995.

PLACES TO VISIT

The following gardens are accessible to the public, some openly, others by prior arrangement or on specified dates each year. They all hold some connection to Repton or are discussed in this book, even if he was not directly responsible for their layout.

Ashridge Estate, Visitor Centre, Moneybury Hill, Ringshall, near Berkhamsted, Hertfordshire HP4 1LX.
   Telephone: 01442 851227. Website: www.nationaltrust.org.uk/ ashridge-estate (The house is privately owned. To learn more about it, please visit: www.ashridge.org.uk)

Park Campsite, Cannock Wood, Rugeley, Staffordshire WS15 4JJ.
   Telephone: 01543 682278. Website: www.beaudesert.org

Berrington Hall, near Leominster, HR6 0DW.
   Telephone: 01568 615721. Website: www.nationaltrust.org.uk/ berrington-hall

Blaise Castle Estate, Kings Weston Road, Lawrence Weston, Bristol BS10 7QS. Telephone: 0117 9639174.
   Website: www.bristol.gov.uk/page/leisure-and-culture/blaise-castle-estate (The folly castle is opened on occasion by volunteers, or visit the Blaise Castle House Museum, Henbury Road, Henbury, Bristol

BS10 7QS. Telephone: 0117 9039818.)

Brighton Royal Pavilion, 4/5 Pavilion Buildings, Brighton BN1 1EE.
  Telephone: 03000 290900. Website: www.brighton-hove-rpml.org.uk

Catton Hall, in the village of Old Catton, north of Norwich.
  Website: www.cattonpark.com (Repton's very first commission
  for Jeremiah Ives survives as a Grade II-listed public park.)

Chatsworth, Bakewell, Derbyshire DE45 1PP.
  Telephone: 01246 565300. Website: www.chatsworth.org

Chiswick House & Gardens Trust, Chiswick House, London W4 2QN.
  Telephone: 0208 7423905. Website: www.chgt.org.uk

Dullingham House, Dullingham, near Newmarket, Cambridgeshire
  CB8 9UP. Telephone: 01638 508186.
  Website: www.ngs.org.uk/gardens/gardenfinder/garden.
  aspx?id=14681 (Visits strictly by appointment with Sir Michael
  and Lady Nourse.)

Felbrigg Hall, Felbrigg, Norwich NR11 8PR. Telephone: 01263 837444.
  Website: www.nationaltrust.org.uk/felbrigg-hall

Harewood House, Harewood, Leeds LS17 9LG. Telephone: 0113 2181010.
  Website: www.harewood.org

Hatchlands Park, East Clandon, Guildford, Surrey GU4 7RT.
  Telephone: 01483 222482. Website: www.nationaltrust.org.uk/
  hatchlands-park

Holkham Hall, Wells-next-the-Sea, Norfolk NR23 1AB.
  Telephone: 01328 710227. Website: www.holkham.co.uk

Hotel Endsleigh, Milton Abbot, Tavistock, Devon PL19 0PQ.
  Telephone: 01822 870000. Website: www.hotelendsleigh.com

Leigh Court, Leigh Court Business Centre, Abbots Leigh, Bristol BS8 3RA.
  Telephone: 01275 373393. Website: www.leighcourt.co.uk

Longleat, Warminster, Wiltshire BA12 7NW. Telephone: 01985 844400.
  Website: www.longleat.co.uk/explore/longleat-house

Moccas Court, Moccas, Herefordshire HR2 9LH. Telephone: 01981 500019.
  Website: www.moccas-court.co.uk

Montgomery Place, 25 Gardener Way, Red Hook, New York 12504, USA.
  Website: www.hudsonvalley.org/historic-sites/montgomery-place

Plas Newydd Country House and Gardens, Llanfairpwll LL61 6DQ.
  Telephone: 01248 714795. Website: www.nationaltrust.org.uk/
  plas-newydd

Rippon Lea House & Gardens, 192 Hotham Street, Elsternwick, Victoria
  3185, Australia.
  Website: www.ripponleaestate.com.au

Rode Hall, Scholar Green, Cheshire ST7 3QP. Telephone: 01270 873237.
  Website: www.rodehall.co.uk

Sheringham Park, Upper Sheringham, Norfolk NR26 8TL.
Telephone: 01263 820550. Website: www.nationaltrust.org.uk/
sheringham-park

Stoneleigh Abbey, Kenilworth, Warwickshire CV8 2LF.
Telephone: 01926 858535/858585. Website: www.stoneleighabbey.org

Stowe, Buckingham MK18 5EQ. Telephone: 01280 817156.
Website: www.nationaltrust.org.uk/stowe

Sufton Court, Mordiford, Herefordshire HR1 4LU.
Telephone: 01432 870268.
Website: www.hha.org.uk/Property/407/Sufton-Court

Tatton Park, Knutsford, Cheshire, WA16 6QN. Telephone: 01625 374400.
Website: www.tattonpark.org.uk

The Trentham Estate, Stone Road Trentham, Stoke-on-Trent, Staffordshire
ST4 8AX. Telephone: 01782 646646.
Website: www.trentham.co.uk

Thoresby Hall Hotel, Thoresby Park, near Ollerton, Nottinghamshire
NG22 9WH. Telephone: 01623 82100.
Website: www.warnerleisurehotels.co.uk/hotels/thoresby-hall-hotel

Welbeck, Welbeck Estates Company Ltd, Cavendish House, Welbeck,
Worksop, Nottinghamshire S80 3LL. Telephone: 01909 500211.
Website: www.welbeck.co.uk

Wimpole Hall, Arrington, Royston SG8 0BW. Telephone: 01223 206000.
Website: www.nationaltrust.org.uk/wimpole-estate

Woburn Abbey, Woburn, Bedfordshire MK17 9WA.
Telephone: 01525 290333.
Website: www.woburn.co.uk

INDEX